C000135474

In loving memory of Alison Mackay

1951—2009

The Weepers

Lindsay Macgregor

CALDER WOOD PRESS

2015

The Weepers by Lindsay Macgregor

Published by **Calder Wood Press**

1 Beachmont Court, Dunbar, EH42 1YF, UK

www.calderwoodpress.co.uk

ISBN: 978-1-902629-58-2

Acknowledgements are due to the editors of the following publications in which some of the poems in this pamphlet first appeared: *New Writing Scotland, Northwords Now, Poetry Scotland.* and the anthology *Seagate III,* edited by A. Jackson.

Landnám was highly commended in the 2013 William Soutar poetry competition.

My thanks to Jayne Wilding of Fife and Dundee Maggie's Centres who introduced me to writing and so changed the course of my life. Grateful thanks also to my tutors, Kirsty Gunn and Jim Stewart, of the University of Dundee Writing Practice and Study programme for their generous and insightful advice and support. Thank you to my friends in Edinburgh and Dundee writing groups who have read versions of these poems over the years. I am indebted to the Scottish Book Trust for a New Writer's Award in 2015 and I am grateful to Colin Will, editor at Calder Wood Press, for his patience and thoughtfulness. Finally, my thanks to my friends and family and to Margaret, Alan and Alison Mackay.

Printed by MDPD, Musselburgh

Landnám

According to lost sources
she appeased her gods
with spills of salt at rockfall
beneath fowling cliffs,
a touch of metal
for protection from men
who knelt to face
the coldest hill.

With words as callous
as the waves,
she pinned compass
points to air — *Symbister, Wasbister,
Isbister, Norbister* —
time twisting sounds
to suit its fish-eyed self.

They say she even named
the space between the walls,
regardless of what went
before, in certain knowledge
wood and stone
are not the same
as home and nothing
can't be mapped.

The Weepers I

She muttered, *Scatter*
my ashes in these six places,
then digressed into a coma,
watched over by a flock
of golden psychopomps.

First, a sea where men in flags
of black are tied to mizzen
masts; secondly, a loch
which Artemis has walked
upon; third, the hunting

ground of Hecate; fourth,
a fatherland of fallacies
and cemeteries; fifth,
a desert parting of the ways;
sixth, a stellar nursery.

Lymphoedema

For nigh on twenty years I came back
from the Fishing Rock with creels
of line-caught ling and cod
to lick the salt from folds of skin
between her toes until the day
I found her hauled up on a spit of sand,
her orbit eyes staring at stars
pouring from the sky into a sea unseen
beyond the broken line of the horizon.

I fed her morsels. She swallowed
stones. Her body, pierced with silver
hooks, took on water, faded
to a mottle. Within the week
a red-raw hole broke in her abdomen,
a harpoon wound, her legs had fused,
her webbed feet formed a single fin
as she waited for the tide to turn.

Association of Women Clerks and Secretaries (AWCS)

Those queens of cigarettes and ginger wine
were often bought by men
with brittle flowers for buttonholes.

No two were alike
despite the fine painted lines, their insistence
on outcrops and ledges, the diets of fish,

their refusal to nest.
Many were clubbed till they loosened their feathers,
flightless, ready for death.

They could never have flourished
in Arctic conditions.
They'd be taken for witches.

Now, addled in shallows,
they follow the wake
of the garefowl.

The Weepers II

I searched for the giveaway signs
of a broch where the road became fog,
where drizzle hardened to rain:
on a mound by the lochan,
a lintel, a hearth and a trough.

Through the door came
the Weepers - a prophet,
a shepherd, a spinner, a fisher,
a nine-year old child,
a woman reeking of drink.

We walked over the edge
of the jubilant cliff, drawn to
the pink of the thrift,
the cormorant's
miracle nest.

Bog People

The scene is set.
Hinds heckle rain as one last fawn
floats like a floating burlap sack
upon a stagnant pool.

She knows hill dwellers salvage
what they can, quern-stones, crucks,
wishbones for a lower life.

He watches water
clearfell lynchets, drag
the seven Ransom Stones
across the submerged barley field;
fails to recognise the scent of sedge
or cotton grass before he makes amends.

Sundews close rank on puckered flesh.
Sphagnum holds between dissolving bones.

Wortcunning

The floor of the forest's a larder
for lepers and orphans of cottars
who swallowed the sleep thorns
with dodder and madder then woke
to the voices of gargoyles or gremlins
and true tales of ravens that roosted
on ogres who stole Saint Veronica's
monikered handkerchief stitched by
her stepmother's stepmother's stepmother.

The Weepers III

She'd stipulated Sanna Bay
on a sunny day, approached
from the volcano. Half-way there
the woman knocking back the valium
and vodkas finds stuff falling out of cliffs –

building stone, bone combs, fragments
she called gaming pieces, empty
razorshells. She reckoned Viking Age
(though the Weepers begged to differ).
Probably the gable-end of a longhouse

and its midden. She spoke about the time
she found a burial – a child, a man,
an older woman – in a boat,
with a sword, a shield and a spinning
wheel. But what intrigued her most

were the metal rivets still intact
where the softwood planks
had rotted. She'd lived with violence
far too long. No wonder she'd acquired
a taste for anchovies. The evening sun

was licking up the sand. We walked
a mile or more along the shore,
her sucking on her unlit pipe.
She pointed to a heap
of wrack. In amongst the tiny

crisp black bladders,
a human skull, blanched
by wind and sea. She said
she hadn't told the Police.
She said it wasn't Archaeology.

The Weepers ground the skull
to dust which she mixed
with her tobacco. I scrambled
over slipshod rocks of roosting
guillemots to offer cinders

to the sea. They gyred above
the breaking waves like a genie
or a trace of smoke
from a pyre of softwood planks.
Or a troubled woman's pipe.

Crex crex

At first he makes her heart
vibrate, names himself
in midnight fricatives.

Soon, she hears him
scraping flakes of Mesolithic
flint across a bunch of hazel

twigs but knows it's futile
trying to raise a spark
in tall, damp meadow grass

despite the spires of yellow flags.
She's mildly irritated now.
Oblivious, he carries on

his dull compulsion. Frankly,
she would rather hear a dirty story,
wishes he would change

his twisted tune. It's not for love
that she relents then dreams
of Africa in perfect silence.

The Lewis Chesswoman

She knows she's just a dolled-up
pawn to him. Slugs more mead.
Recites the game-plan in her head,
rehearses every sideways move.
How she'd love to go berserk
with mitts like these, his bishops
putting shame to shame. Instead,
it's constant stalemate.

The Weepers IV

Glen Lee in early February,
the Weepers and the Relict
rivalling the waning moon
for taciturnity. Did no one think
to ring the Passing Bell?

We navigate by withered leaves
beyond the reconstructed keep
where freezing fog and falling snow
lay everything to sleeping ghosts
and winding sheets (except the crimson

blood and pluck of a gralloched hind
oozing through soft rime).
By the time we reach the boathouse
door, the herd has moved across
the moor. Weepers aren't worth

their salt these days. The Loch's still
locked beneath its crust. I chisel
through resistant ice, strew
ashes to the open wound -
they radiate like the movement

of the herd across the moor.
The drift attracts a shoal
of browsing Arctic charr. I let them
feed, then, fishing deep, I net them.
We must eat.

St. Maelrubha's Feast Day, Loch Maree

Take my advice, with the farrier of Slioch gone
six summers past, don't row alone
across the hallowed loch of the moon goddess
to an island on an island.

In the hermitage of hazel trees, don't stoop
to read the gravestones of the furnacemen,
the Red McLeods, their lives reduced,
like healing wells, to little more than rumour.

Don't place your hope in the buckled oak,
its rags and ribbons, two bone buttons,
pilgrims' tarnished coins – copper's
killed the patron saint of love-sick lunatics.

A Chafing Dish

Umpteen years she'd catered for
the Shooting Lodge – rook pie,
calf's heid, a bit of potted hough.
Come August she'd be called upon
to carve the larded guinea fowl
she'd drawn, plucked and singed.
As a rule, she'd carefully remove
the merry-thought, though not,

of course, the crop. That is,
until the day she boned
two dozen larks and stuffed them
with a farce containing fragments
of his late lamented lordship's
favourite claret glass.
She put it down to misadventure
or an accident of class.

18

Great Skua

On land you look banished,
in thrall to the heather,
nostalgic for battle
with jarls from the sagas,
you clodhopper,
built like a barrel

or something the tusker
threw up.

When you take to the air, it's sackcloth
and ashes, the sail of a longship
bound for Valhalla,
ambushing gannets
with kennings and eddas
until they surrender,

then drowning
a fulmar for love.

The Weepers V

We've spooled in single file
across the gorge
while hoopoes call
as though they know
the source of every river.

The Weepers breach
an entrance to the cave
where a child insists she lives
six months a year. Above our heads,
a colony of horseshoe bats makes

shadows in the dark.
We hold our breath, lose
our bearings in underwater
chambers, track the sound
of droplets dripping into

grottos, follow clawmarks
up the walls of galleries
with memories of predators
and prey until the passage
gets too narrow to continue.

We'll have to send the child.
While the Weepers gather
charcoal abandoned by
Neanderthals, I mix the ash
with yellow ochre, hematite

and spit. The child crawls
down the funnelled shaft,
illuminates the outline of a turtle,
hind quarters of a horse
breaking out of fissures in the rock.

She traces pigment
round her fingers, daubs
geometric signs, extending
genealogy with sympathetic
magic of the single human line.

Ethel

Meanwhile, dying on the day ward, it's only
the world authority on Mesozoic echinoids,
re-enacting her discovery of mammoth tusks
in fine dark clay (though the ivory
was much decayed) near Bishopriggs,

the animal's most northerly location.
She surmised that reindeer crossed
the Forth-Clyde line on floating ice. Then died.
The men, of course, were not amused.
Her lack of chaperones. Her shabby shoes.

CSI

A dyke like her who's been around the block
a bit has heard it all before. Volcano, somewhere
near the Tropics, unexpectedly collapses. Tuffs,
the only witnesses, suspiciously fall in. So,

she's been doing forensics on her knees,
dusting prints of giant centipedes in seams
of limestone six foot thick. She's taken
statements from the alibis whose stories

never tally – brachiopods, trilobites,
crinoid stems, coral cups – recorded them
like ripple marks in rock. Then cordoned
off a cove where shifty-looking water

flowed and, sure enough, it blabbed
about the time when sand slid down
the shallow slopes below the old sea cliff.
Soon she had sandstone, siltstone, even

Dolomitic limestone queuing up to give
their versions. She shifted shingle
on the shore for any signs of slickensides
before her final tour de force. Who turned

sticky mudstone into clay? In unison,
they pin the blame on rain. But she's
got all the evidence she needs
and brings them all to book.

Miss Petrie

On buttermilk Sundays,
thirled to the stoup
of St. Perdita's kirk,

straining stale water
from vases of lilies,
Miss Petrie surrenders

to ramsons and sorrel,
the floor of the forest,
the charcoal, the clinker,

the embers, the rust.
Even buttermilk
curdles when cursed.

The Weepers VI

Nearing the end, she wants
to bring her father back
with a compass in his collar
stud, his handlebar
moustache. The Prophet's

in the cockpit, Weepers
for his Wingmen, clamouring for
night attacks on Dresden, Leipzig,
the bombing of the Ruhr.
The starboard engine's

packing in. I should have
been a farmer. It's
name, rank and number
to Dulag Luft. Sagan. Four days in,
the Prophet's in the cooler,

plotting our escape,
saving Red Cross packing
cases, modifying tins of Klim
for oxygen, bartering
the last two Gold Flake

cigarettes he'd captured
at Dunkirk. I'm shoring
up the tunnels underneath
the yard while Weepers
vault the wooden horse, hide

documents in Thunder Boxes,
learning what it means
to be a man. By night we mingle
yellow sand with ashes of
the children of the war-dead.

Rowan

(after *Discs moving into Dark Green, Wilhelmina Barns-Graham*)

I keep a woman in my closet
amongst my canisters
of mustard gas, the forest
green of battle dress,
outdated geometric shapes.
She keeps me out of kilter,
my familiar.

The Weepers VII

The Weepers follow clawmarks
of a limping, three-toed
Allosaurus, divining copper
ores along the Moab fault.
Even water's petrified

by proselytising pioneers
praying for a deluge.
Here comes the one
we're waiting for.
She's herding bighorn sheep,

domesticating mule deer,
mountain chickadees.
She's been tried
for cattle rustling,
brewing beer and brandy

out of apricots and chokeberries
in Prohibition time.
She should have watched
her children when the Mormon
crickets swarmed.

Now we're mixing ash
with axle grease, remembering
the names of everyone who's ever
died of gunshot wounds or mortal
pox at Independence Rock.

Mother Lode

All gold is born angry as ripgut
and mustard, those weeds
of the New World that grow in the alleys
of Hangtown and Jackson –
you can bet every building's a peepshow
or brothel, its cards on the table,
gun-toting coyotes panhandling
the backyards in duck pants,
red flannels and panama hats.
It's a stitch-up or a stick-up
and everyone's guilty
in Hangtown and Jackson
except for sweet Lola Montez.

Cudknot

Year upon year, she mowed the back lawn,
Backward and forward, come hell or high water.

Thirty years on, she looked past the fence
To a paddock of cudknot and fescues – a mess.

So she mowed down the field till she blunted the blades
Then she shoved and shunted; she started again.

Out past the pond to the lip of the river,
She striped every meadow from Ceres to Cupar.

In a year and a half she got out to the cliffs,
Left a strewing of purslane and sheepsbit and thrift.

The look in her eye pierced the eye of each daisy
Through Cornwall, past Roskoff and into the valleys

And hills of the Causse, she kept cutting those swards
And cutting and cutting and still there was more

To be mown, more to be mown as she mowed
And she mowed on right out of this world.

The Weepers VIII

On day eight of delirium
there's talk of gannets,
Dunnet Head, a thirst that can't
be quenched. Long-tailed
birds with human heads

have settled round the bed
as though they were the meek.
She makes a necklace
of their beaks and imitates
their silent song. I turn

the mirrors to the wall, invite
the brutal chaplain in to say
a final word. He wants to know
what lies ahead. She mouths
Our mother's death and sends

him packing with the rest.
So now there's only me
and her. She whispers,
Throw whatever's left
to the Horsehead Nebula.

As the words sink in, I picture me,
the Weepers and a shaman
off our heads on mescaline,
spinning through Earth's
atmosphere, past meteors

and shooting stars,
near-missing minor planets,
to the coral glow of hydrogen
and helium, and the last
eclipse of Zeta Heraclis.

Fairfax Somerville

Not being a Cambridge man,
she knew the distance
of Venus from the Sun.
Birds ate from her mouth
as she proved god's
existence by differential
calculus. While they preached
against her name in York
Cathedral, she was boiling
quantities of marmalade
for Sir Edward Parry's
voyage to an island
so far north, it slipped
beyond all memory of snow.

Herschel

While he was at the eyepiece,
shouting observations,
his little sister practised

arias from Judas Maccabeus
and made the calculation,
standing on a stool,

that no matter the condition
of the skies around Andromeda
and Cetus, she would ride

to Greenwich with her catalogue
of comets, her argument for
women minding heaven.

The Book of Jean

She scries a reliquary of words,
fills it with spills of tiny starfish
stuccoed into sediment,
soft parts long lost in water's
thirst for salt. She sprinkles
it with seeds of meadowsweet,
buttercup, forget-me-not,
pressed like sickle cells into
her article of faith, wood shavings
from a stillborn's cradle splashed
across the impress of the wingbeat
of a plover, in remembrance of some
summer, her elegy in umber.

After Life

It makes little odds if you've tended the light of St. Lucy
on Scotland's Most Northerly Rock like an acolyte
shipwrecked at dawn in a Dark Age
or whether you've spent your days living as Lilith, widowing
souls of the nine Fallen Women on islands where only
the Grass of Parnassus grows tall by intemperate lochs.
When you come to the end of your story,
you'll either be hearing confessions of penitent priests
on their knees or sweeping the cobwebs under
the carpet in everyday deathbed scenes.
As the Duty Nurse closes your lids
with her palms in a last benediction,
you're hoping for laurels and trumpets in heaven
or devils on horseback in hell. What you never expected
was this

The Weepers IX

We've poured the earthly
remnants of her body
to the elements (though
Weepers claim that nebulae
are straining credibility). It's time

to call a halt. The spinner,
shepherdess and alcoholic,
fisherwoman, child
and prophet take
their proper places

in the mantle
of the broch before
the final strewing
of the ashes through the pages
of this book. Dismiss

the psychotherapists,
the suffragists, the satirists;
dismiss the Resurrectionists,
Revivalists, Redemptionists.
There's nothing to be done.

Notes

The Weepers – professional mourners

Landnám – Old Norse, settlement (Viking Age settlement of Iceland, Faroe, Northern and Western Isles)

Symbister, Wasbister, Isbister, Norbister: Old Norse bólstaðr farm divisions in Orkney and Shetland.

Wortcunning – knowledge of properties of plants

Garefowl – Great auk

Crex crex – corncrake

Dulag Luft - Prisoner of War interrogation centre near Frankfurt-am-Main, Germany

Sagan – POW camp in Poland for Air Force prisoners captured during the Second World War

Klim – wartime brand of powdered milk

Ethel – Ethel Currie, 1899-1963, Scottish palaeontologist

Fairfax Somerville – Mary Fairfax Somerville, 1780 – 1872, Scottish astronomer and mathematician

Herschel – Caroline Herschel , 1750-1848, astronomer and singer